NOT FOR FLOWERS

a hundred villanelle sonnets

AUTHOR
Cláudia Cassoma
www.claudiacassoma.com

TITLE
~~Not~~ For Flowers

FOREWORD
Tuere Anne Marshall

IMAGE ON THE COVER
Selina Leunert

GRAPHIC COMPOSITION
Cláudia Cassoma / Kujikula

PUBLISHER
Kujikula
kujikula@gmail.com

ISBN: 9781732665316

1st Edition — March 8th, 2019
2nd Edition — March 8th, 2022

All Rights Reserved.
© 2022 Cláudia Cassoma & Kujikula

NOT FOR FLOWERS

CLÁUDIA CASSOMA

there
will not be
change
until
all voices
are heard

to my
mom,
for being
the strongest
and most
beautiful
flower
i have ever known

to my
little
sisters,
for
brightening
my world
and inspiring
my actions

make
yourself
heard

FOREWORD

Tuere Anne Marshall

FOREWORD

"When the student is ready the teacher will appear" has been my motto for the past decades teaching, tutoring, and mentoring students from my faculty position in departments of English. It has been a passion of mine to teach who ever enters my classroom whether it's the composition classes, developmental courses, grammar workshops, or literature of the diaspora. However, my absolute joy is to teach the nuances of literary expressions our great authors have produced. Each year I am taught new connections my students unpack to ancient and contemporary poems, short stories, or novels.

Cláudia Cassoma was one of those students who entered my classroom and demonstrated an understanding of world literature and a passion for the arts, which confirmed my calling to teach. This fifth book of poetry by Cláudia – her first written in English – takes the reader on a pastoral journey as she poetically expresses emotions that many of us feel, but cannot articulate. Beginning with "desert-rose," the reader will flow into Claudia's world of creating a "new spring" through courage. The creativity in each poem combines the formality of the villanelle's structure with the artistic fluidity found in life. Cláudia carved images of beauty and power from dark experiences and joy from the bright moments, as she writes, "well wrapped in a rainbow hug." Awesome image. Her art touches the vulnerable places of identity, friendship, solitude, death, courage, love, intimacy, femininity – all the vicissitudes of our lives.

~~NOT~~ FOR FLOWERS is a refreshing addition to the libraries of literature and a must read for all who want to understand the myriad facets one encounters. Ms. Cassoma's creativity will guide you. It will give me an abundance of joy to present this volume of poems from one of our new and great authors to my students in anticipation of the discussions it is sure to generate. The next generation of learners now have a poetic roadmap in ~~NOT~~ FOR FLOWERS to find for themselves new way to express the bright and dark moments life promises. Thank you, Cláudia, for this exciting book of villanelle poetry.

Peace, Joy, and Health
Tuere Anne Marshall

PREFACE

"Women are like flowers"

I grew up hearing that line. Unquestionably lived the only acceptable meaning of that *truth*. It was in all places, and belonged to *all* of us. *It's so **you** to be gentle, no one else can do it* – that was the lesson. Some grew up knowing that would be their place. They too would sit there. Their tenderness would not be *wasted* anywhere else. Time and again, we saw the one-item-menu circulating at the hands of women everywhere. I read it at one point: sit near *their* table, and make sure your gentleness betters *their* lives. That was the serving. For the longest time, we *all* did just that. Eventually, I didn't. Maybe I lost the taste for it, I don't know for sure. But please, before you go unleashing your horses, hear me well: I never claimed that there was anything wrong with being a flower. Never that! I just started to question whether there was more to it: Are we flowers? Are there different kinds? If so, can I choose to be more than one?

As luck would have it, I had always been a major aromaphilic. I just can't help but sniff all around. I also happen to like flowers quite a bit. And while I might've silenced my actions, I never disregarded my curiosity. So, with all speed, I embarked on a quest. First, to understand what they meant by that line. Then, to understand *why*.

~~Not~~ **For Flowers** is a collection of essays in the size of sonnets with voices of women I met along the way – and my own. From what we heard to what we saw. From what we had to what we wanted. From what we did to what we felt. We even dared to think of the future.

The necessity of compiling this report, arose from my own uneasiness with respect to how women are seen. I wanted to repave the grounds for my sisters. Then, it amounted to worries beyond mine. Revealed secrets we shared. Became the start of a much longer conversation. The gathering of evolving minds – *our* respective minds. And the home base for the redefining of each of our lives.

~~Not~~ **For Flowers** is a way to celebrate and build up the goals of March 8th. What's more, it is a way to do that every day. Each villanelle is a step far beyond the annual pink parties and the feminal songs. It is progress!

Cláudia Cassoma

TO WOMEN AND GIRLS EVERYWHERE

(and to everyone else)

I write to you with a filled heart. Time came and time passed. In the present tense, on the shadows of my footprints, I have the trail that brought me here. On the mountains of my cheekbones, I have the tears that dried up. I still hold some of the stones I picked up along the way and remember the stories that sounded too familiar. So, I'll speak of them. I'll reveal lines of many. Whichever dares go passed my discomfort and land on this page anyway. I will make sure everyone knows. Ears close and ears far will fathom our stories – my sisters' and my own. It will all be here. Or perhaps just some. I doubt I'll be able to completely expose all the truths in my heart, still I'll try. I'll try to open it up honestly and share it clearly, so that, as we go beyond the wonder, we think of better ways. I will do it to the extent that it helps you to hear as much as it does me to say. More importantly, I'll stop. I will mark the paragraph with ellipsis for us all: For women and girls everywhere, and for everyone else.

My dear, this is not a letter where I attempt to suppose your thoughts, theorize your feelings, nor do I desire to define your entire life merely because I too have a vagina. No. I recognize and respect our differences. I know this is not all voices, but it's a beginning. Having said that, I am also writing to you that is nothing like me.

Time and again, we were fed all sorts of life ideals. They told us that our worth was in the way we adorned our bodies – as in what we *chose* to do with it. Some of us trusted them enough to think that was actually true. The *only* truth. So, we decided to have our figures just like they wanted; we accepted to live with their pleasures.

Our entire lives, we rendered ourselves valuable, desirable, and even useful, based solely on the size of our dresses and the silence in our mouths. We reduced the size of our plates in an effort to feel better about ourselves when confronted by the reflection staring back at us in the mirror. We let ourselves be defined in relation to others and not as complete beings on our own. We just let ourselves be defined. Regrettably, we dismissed from our minds the beautiful fact that we can be whatever floats our boat. We absorbed the misleading concept that there's only one truth under which we should all reside. And that was all for not being born with a pointy organ of copulation like theirs. And when we failed to live up to those unrealistic expectations – we rejected ourselves.

I hated myself deeply. There was a time not even my deepest efforts were enough. For reasons imaginable and otherwise, I found no basis to be proud of myself. The first time was when I understood that I was a girl. Not because I wanted to be something else, rather because I fully grasped the anguish of it all. I saw the challenges from afar. I never blamed anyone; I still don't. Those that I could perhaps justly blame, had the same reality, I understood.

I understood why I took the blame for defending myself from the testosterone filled teenager challenging my existence. I understood why I made myself invisible when in their sights. I covered myself up so they didn't sin. That was my life. I hid the strength of my will and ignored my doubts. And I never protested. I just stood there - I understood.

I understood why she insisted on telling me that I would be a better woman shutting my mouth, closing my legs, and cleaning. When I understood what I wanted to be, and realized what I was, I already hated myself too much. It suddenly hit me that, in their eyes, being a flower wasn't so much about the beauty; the strength, the resilience, and other many things that the real ones were.

The ability to be docile and the contrary; to exist in the winter just as well as in the spring breeze; to enjoy both the red and the black of life was ~~not~~ for flowers.

Some of us heard about the *need* to sprout and how we *should* all aspire to it. We were told that we were only biology and we believed it. Please understand: I just wish it wasn't given to as *the* only definition. And not to the little ones. Never that! Consequently we were robbed of your chemistry. Some very early in life. Others a bit later. Eventually, many were made senseless. Let me repeat: I don't wish to speculate on how you feel about your mothers and grandmother's relics. Nor am I advocating for blunt disrespect. I just want to make sure you are living your own dreams. Nothing would make me happier than hearing that from you. Are you happy?

Rather than presume your truths, I would like to see them in you. Rather than projecting my wanting, I wish to see your happiness splashed across your face. Your smile as the true testament of your fulfillment. Please, don't think of me as moralistic, it's not that at all.

It has taken forever for us to shape our own existence. Our past has limited us long enough; our present has been too averse; and our futures are still too dicey, we simply must start looking for our own answers.

When one has successfully robbed a human the ability to think and to question, they have, by all odds, ended a life. So, I'm glad we started thinking just in time.

This letter is to you. You that is still lost in the many conflicting ideals, perhaps unhealthy and, at times, slaying, that the world imposes upon us. You that is still figuring out who to be, while the world throws its own standards. You that still lives the hatred of before, while missing your inborn beauty. You that wants to change.

I did say before, this is not a selfish endeavor to suppose your thoughts, theorize your feelings, or define your life. Just eagerness to know whether you are happy. If you have found your voice, your very own beginning.

This is to women and girls everywhere, and to everyone else. To those who rose to a different truth; one that entails leveled self-esteem, self-confidence, self-reliance, self-fulfillment, and a high dose of equity.

This is to you, mom. It is my way of thanking you for being such an example of bravery and resilience; for showing the face of strength and the body of a capable human being – all while acknowledging your pain.

This is to you two as well, Antónia e Nassoma. It's my attempt to obviate all reasons for you to ever hate yourselves. This is me paving the way. Though we'll still share this world, I hope you have way better experiences.

• • •

For change,
Cláudia Cassoma

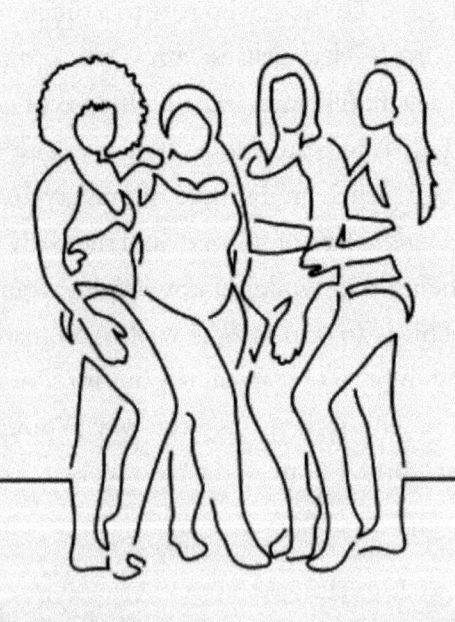

together
is so much
better

GRATITUDE

Cláudia Cassoma

Creating this book was a truly undreamt odyssey.

I am grateful to Professor Marshall for joining me in this journey and sowing words of confidence along my path. Kevin Milton, the terrific friend life was so gracious as to give me, thank you so much for helping me polish the lines of this compendium of earthshaking villanelles.

To my partner, Mark, everlasting thanks for the priceless support you have always been. I love you dearly.

Do not believe for a second that I forgot about you. Yes, you clamant friends. You've been bugging me for a book in this weird language for far too long. Well, I hope you're happy now. Go on and enjoy yourself. Feel free to ask for seconds. It's really your fault I wrote this.

And I hope you too experience an eventful read!

be
whatever
kind of
flower
you
aspire to
be

NOT FOR FLOWERS

DESERT ROSE

as a new spring is born i flourish
never ashamed of what i went through
cause what you see is my own courage

i told myself not to perish
and, before long, ignited anew
as a new spring is born i flourish

there was no God to care and nourish
now proudness runs along my tissue
cause what you see is my own courage

here with steady purpose
since alone i grew
as a new spring is born i flourish

as a new spring is born I flourish
cause what you see is my own courage

FLOURISH

dress yourself up with a selfish desire
do not fear being the only one
and let that zeal be what takes you higher

rough roads, lonely moments, perhaps fire
none of that means you are done
dress yourself up with a selfish desire

as your high heels set out to tire
remember why you begun
and let that zeal be what takes you higher

go with what your fears aspire
and like you never felt undone
dress yourself up with a selfish desire

dress yourself up with a selfish desire
and let that zeal be what takes you higher

AMARYLLIS BELLADONNA

her beauty is on the face she wears
her ruttish eyes, her willing lips
is on what runs through her brain

the way she goes up the stairs
somewhere beyond her killer hips
her beauty is on the face she wears

she's got no chain
her beauty is before her fingertips
is on what runs through her brain

she goes over your ignorance amain
being the flower she herself nips
her beauty is on the face she wears

her beauty is on the face she wears
is on what runs through her brain

HOME

no fear, peace near, a world ever crystal clear
behind swollen breasts, within a cozy hollow
  floating on the only red that's not death

  underneath the heart that holds me dear
in brightened sphere, in spite road so narrow
no fear, peace near, a world ever crystal clear

 closed eyes, curled legs, a very merry breath
kicking as i'm warm, hope is what i swallow
  floating on the only red that's not death

  "life of mine" – her voice is what i hear
"no monsters here" – ease is where i wallow
no fear, peace near, a world ever crystal clear

no fear, peace near, a world ever crystal clear
  floating on the only red that's not death

I'LL BE RIGHT HERE

when you realize that you were never made heaven
when your bare mind understands that i always was
that this hubris belief is nothing more than your fear

although you have forged, no power was ever given
you'll see that i've been even despite the tardy laws
when you realize that you were never made heaven

when the day comes, i'll be here as it becomes clear
as you see that i was way before this enabling clause
that this hubris belief is nothing more than your fear

despite life's unfair divides, i'll protect my essence
you'll see i'm not doing for a mere phallic applause
when you realize that you were never made heaven

when you realize that you were never made heaven
that this hubris belief is nothing more than your fear

PERENNIAL SELF

may you reflect the one that resides in you
may you render yourself entire
every time your two feet touch the ground

as today goes and moonlight becomes due
and you check what you desire
may you reflect the one that resides in you

if you ever feel pressured by what's around
fight like you are a class-c fire
every time your two feet touch the ground

when you look around and friends are few
despite fearing all could expire
may you reflect the one that resides in you

may you reflect the one that resides in you
every time your two feet touch the ground

BIRD OF PARADISE

let it hurt
but, please, hold on
you'll feel joy at last

rain is just another way to start
there's rainbow once it's gone
let it hurt

don't wait to be asked
do as you dream upon
you'll feel joy at last

don't you ever cease to assert
and if they delay the dawn
let it hurt

let it hurt
you'll feel joy at last

DEADLY SIN

as i go, my soles leave self-respect and personal worth
regardless of their insistence to convince me otherwise
it's clear i'm walking with a lot of it, and i do not care

since i understood the exact meaning of my bitter birth
unafraid, i live like i too would evolve into butterflies
as i go, my soles leave self-respect and personal worth

"one day such complacence will leave your spring bare"
—so they curse, but way before hitting my ears it dies
it's clear i'm walking with a lot of it, and i do not care

my pride is concrete, and though i might soon eat earth
each breath is a genuine step towards my soul's demise
as i go, my soles leave self-respect and personal worth

as i go, my soles leave self-respect and personal worth
it's clear i'm walking with a lot of it, and i do not care

BLUEBIRDS

we dance till the wee hours calm our zesty figures
we laugh as if our bladders were forever young
we are free souls flying to the heart of our dreams

we go proving that we are perpetual glory diggers
we sing songs that have sadly been left unsung
we dance till the wee hours calm our zesty figures

we don't care for their oppressing blaring screams
we don't need to scare, we speak a better tongue
we are free souls flying to the heart of our dreams

we trustingly hold the skirts of our older sisters
we see on their lit eyes the joy that has sprung
we dance till the wee hours calm our zesty figures

we dance till the wee hours calm our zesty figures
we are free souls flying to the heart of our dreams

LETTER TO A FORMER EXUBERANT SOUL

dear flower, i know winter is trying to wipe you out
bringing thy whites down on you with no mercy
but you only have to trust that spring is just around

soon it will color and you'll be free from any doubt
you just can't forget that you are still too worthy
dear flower, i know winter is trying to wipe you out

you may not yet see the joy that's your soul's gown
now, only dismay seems to be coming in a hurry
but you only have to trust that spring is just around

life is a lot more than what makes your fear shout
although it is hurting like there's no lord to thee
dear flower, i know winter is trying to wipe you out

dear flower, i know winter is trying to wipe you out
but you only have to trust that spring is just around

INTIMATE COVENANT

i'll let a smile wake me up, that'll be my own
i'll assure i recognize the one in the mirror
the color of my dress will be solid me

no fear will push me away from dawn
no other false breath will destroy my inner
i'll let a smile wake me up, that'll be my own

as sun resumes and i ready for bunches to see
as i go by them with a skin that's a winner
the color of my dress will be solid me

every day i'll build up my own throne
every step will be a mark of my in hero
i'll let a smile wake me up, that'll be my own

i'll let a smile wake me up, that'll be my own
the color of my dress will be solid me

ALL HEART GIVEN

she would call me dear
sometimes i'd have her near
only life was a self-acceptance fear

i recall striving to let myself appear
those days are still so clear
she would call me dear

gradually no more tear
there was some hope to hear
only life was a self-acceptance fear

there's the time that was almost here
the story that'd been sincere
she would call me dear

she would call me dear
only life was a self-acceptance fear

LULLABY

outside will often dim, but know you're the glint
your persistence is exactly what it needs
baby girl, you can trust this song

some steps will face up a flint
and you'll stop to count prayer beads
outside will often dim, but know you're the glint

if you ever weep and pain seems to be too long
look inside for true happiness' seeds
baby girl, you can trust this song

some steps won't face up a flint
and you'll go being the heart that feeds
outside will often dim, but know you're the glint

outside will often dim, but know you're the glint
baby girl, you can trust this song

BE HUMAN

nothing wrong with freeing your soul
getting, giving, dreaming, doing
actions and reactions make you whole

as you grow old and life begins to toll
do all so you don't miss being
nothing wrong with freeing your soul

everything has its own role
laughing, hurting, hating, loving
actions and reactions make you whole

this does not compromise self-control
humans need it all to keep moving
nothing wrong with freeing your soul

nothing wrong with freeing your soul
actions and reactions make you whole

HEATHER

who are you – exceptional being
how to explain your existence
who are you

true sire, fond and farseeing
a pocket with endurance
who are you – exceptional being

so many stories got through
despite means of subsistence
who are you

creating, caring and leading
surely an unlimited brilliance
who are you – exceptional being

who are you – exceptional being
who are you

(IN)STABILITY

commit to memory the festal song of your soul
the one silence that screams when you're alone
    learn to enjoy your own company

free yourself from the hellish thoughts that roll
the joy you are looking for is already your own
commit to memory the festal song of your soul

    repose in soaring wind symphony
    feel like you're not made of bone
    learn to enjoy your own company

liberate minded heart from life's grueling knoll
there's a happier you only waiting to be known
commit to memory the festal song of your soul

commit to memory the festal song of your soul
    learn to enjoy your own company

RAGE

fuel of progressive knees
rolls untiring roaring wheels
full power for unchained minds

slanted hearts it does not please
yet is what the name reveals
fuel of progressive knees

menace for all the blinds
for others, pedestal of steels
full power for unchained minds

more than desire to not appease
much more than good feels
fuel of progressive knees

fuel of progressive knees
full power for unchained minds

REQUIEM FOR INNOCENCE

aware of greater loss, blindness now elegy
no longer interested in seduced innocence
no desire to abide by their partial manifest

forged a place and died to pinkish melody
once dreams made into balanced existence
aware of greater loss, blindness now elegy

high heels, glossy lips, unflinching protest
made exclusive reason of earnest offence
no desire to abide by their partial manifest

erased herself from before-written destiny
freed herself from long-impelled silence
aware of greater loss, blindness now elegy

aware of greater loss, blindness now elegy
no desire to abide by their partial manifest

TRUE FREEDOM

they become their own
not gifted, reclaimed at last
no more shadow to venerate

as they've never shone
unstuck from old past
they become their own

ready pace through the gate
voice, pocket, and now fast
no more shadow to venerate

regardless if they atone
this will finally outlast
they become their own

they become their own
no more shadow to venerate

CRINKLED YOUTH

already a tried existence so early in her spring
left under dark sky, draped in harrowing wind
she sees, she feels, still she chooses to remain

the ones resting on her know they have a king
it might be courage, since life was left behind
already a tried existence so early in her spring

their hunger wets her wraps claiming her gain
crying as she serves they know peace of mind
she sees, she feels, still she chooses to remain

heavy lines in her face are signs of everything
days looking for the light her mom didn't find
already a tried existence so early in her spring

already a tried existence so early in her spring
she sees, she feels, still she chooses to remain

GOD

no doltish mind will ever make sense of you
mediocre eyes won't ever so profoundly see
cause none has successfully explained deity

from nourishing bosom world came through
good, bad, all plunged into sacred milky sea
no doltish mind will ever make sense of you

unending breath for all despite missing fealty
a skirt is something they could never foresee
cause none has successfully explained deity

suffers as their repentance becomes overdue
yet goes being the only GOD to let them free
no doltish mind will ever make sense of you

no doltish mind will ever make sense of you
cause none has successfully explained deity

SOMEWHERE WITHIN

somewhere within the stubborn walls
lips laughing, eyes crying, self being
for her, despite them, upon the world

little girl dancing freedom in the stalls
woman growing unafraid of dreaming
somewhere within the stubborn walls

at long last fair hips felt and swirled
like life was always that good feeling
for her, despite them, upon the world

the sound of the leave that slowly falls
becomes happiness for the time being
somewhere within the stubborn walls

somewhere within the stubborn walls
for her, despite them, upon the world

BROKEN MIND IN RAVISHING BODY

it was never about the way you dressed
with no concealer you were still so fine
your insides never believed, that was it

the tight dress showed you at your best
yet you assumed you could never shine
it was never about the way you dressed

you exist as if faith did a moonlight flit
your say(s) and do(s) never got to align
your insides never believed, that was it

the sun had all to do your soul's behest
alas, your prayers were but a blank line
it was never about the way you dressed

it was never about the way you dressed
your insides never believed, that was it

ORGASMIC BLISS

in sunny days under rainy skies
with all that shakes up my core
well wrapped in a rainbow hug

lost in eminent kiss as god cries
maybe halfway along the shore
in sunny days under rainy skies

with whoever's gentle as a rug
whistling an earth-shaking lore
well wrapped in a rainbow hug

all inattentive to time's disguise
living life as a filled candy store
in sunny days under rainy skies

in sunny days under rainy skies
well wrapped in a rainbow hug

DARE

dare to prove yourself entirely right
blank out ideologies of other minds
dare to think of you as the only one

dare to be your reason to be allright
let you be the luminance that blinds
dare to prove yourself entirely right

dare to do all you want in life's run
progenies, green affairs, do all kinds
dare to think of you as the only one

dare to tone your bold self and fight
go defiantly making wings of winds
dare to prove yourself entirely right

dare to prove yourself entirely right
dare to think of you as the only one

QUEEN ANNE'S LACE

love too, a dose of complexity
an infinite life behind this lace
a blend of that and much more

no false modesty as simplicity
true poetry in unscripted grace
love too, a dose of complexity

an intricate ego, impelled core
gentleness isn't the entire case
a blend of that and much more

a free being exploding ecstasy
leaving beads around the race
love too, a dose of complexity

love too, a dose of complexity
a blend of that and much more

SHORT-SKIRT-BEARING-BODY

wear that damn skirt if you feel like doing so
let the breeze greet your burly legs and even go up
but do remember to take that spray, at least for now

let 'em tell you that you should already know
just don't forget that some's being covered-up
wear that damn skirt if you feel like doing so

you may convince yourself to decor your eyebrow
pour a scent, show cleavage and wear some makeup
but do remember to take that spray, at least for now

i think they're teaching them to interpret a no
fixing mistakes made when things were setup
wear that damn skirt if you feel like doing so

wear that damn skirt if you feel like doing so
but do remember to take that spray, at least for now

ROSE

love your shell just as is, be proud
perfection comes in matchless sizes
ain't nobody out there suchlike you

joy be your body glistening aloud
in need of no comforting disguises
love your shell just as is, be proud

bottom, middle, smile and hair too
known as your own acceptance rises
ain't nobody out there suchlike you

don't dwell on pleasing the crowd
disregard the draining social prizes
love your shell just as is, be proud

love your shell just as is, be proud
ain't nobody out there suchlike you

YEARS DISSEMBLING

more faces than i care to count
lines lost to untrue narrations
loads of way too many deaths

hidden in that better life fount
producing throwaway relations
more faces than i care to count

each sun rise different breaths
brief smiles for false creations
loads of way too many deaths

mirrors with perplexed recount
cause of everyone's reflections
more faces than i care to count

more faces than i care to count
loads of way too many deaths

AGGRAVATED RECALL

gone days make way into my eyes
past ghosts make full new silences
raising dorment tears straightaway

apathetic as fallacious repose dies
as pain becomes suitable absences
gone days make way into my eyes

pleasing lies no longer see the day
die out clarifying bitter differences
raising dorment tears straightaway

coming as active as prodigious skies
binding my soul to forged alliances
gone days make way into my eyes

gone days make way into my eyes
raising dorment tears straightaway

'TIL LIFE DO US PART

my heart will be but yours
its own everlasting zest
'til life do us part

as our thoughts go in pairs
miming a quasi-dual-arrest
my heart will be but yours

every second will be short
you'll lay on my breast
'til life do us part

as long as myself endures
in mind with no alien guest
my heart will be but yours

my heart will be but yours
'til life do us part

STEADY REVERENCE

for the realm that cannot be shaken
considering all which today is ideal
heads bowed manifesting gratitude

as sons that mother didn't forsaken
recognise that she deserves a kneel
for the realm that cannot be shaken

forfeited souls completely renewed
praising highness for plentiful creel
heads bowed manifesting gratitude

with essence that's no longer aching
groveling before the one that's real
for the realm that cannot be shaken

for the realm that cannot be shaken
heads bowed manifesting gratitude

FAREWELL TO INDIFFERENCE

standing on the loam of souls that went down fighting
footprints left as evidence of rage turned into actions
making sure that their progressive efforts still count

auspicious sayings projected to souls barely surviving
dynamic hands spreading truly beneficial convictions
standing on the loam of souls that went down fighting

in their names and for things they couldn't surmount
a conscious disconnect from all stinging distractions
making sure that their progressive efforts still count

so the young knows how tomorrow is now so exciting
short nights readying for the end of all these sanctions
standing on the loam of souls that went down fighting

standing on the loam of souls that went down fighting
making sure that their progressive efforts still count

TO THE GIRL IN THE MIRROR

my love for you is stronger than the most stubborn gales
right here, in the dark of my glary eyes, you're flawless
despite mirror's little desire to reflect your being entire

hair, just as is, face, the smile, each curve, skin, and nails
not even scar preventing me from seeing you as goddess
my love for you is stronger than the most stubborn gales

born in body that's enough, you're all my heart desire
"ever happy" – within few words, a perpetual promise
despite mirror's little desire to reflect your being entire

may you never get lost in world's many depressing tales
you're perfection, look at you, it's no time to be modest
my love for you is stronger than the most stubborn gales

my love for you is stronger than the most stubborn gales
despite mirror's little desire to reflect your being entire

OVERCOME

consent to nothing less than the absolute best
assure each breath a speed of your own want
surmount daringly all fear-made limitations

incapacity perhaps is the screams of the rest
you are better than the weakness they flaunt
consent to nothing less than the absolute best

fill yourself up with the highest expectations
don't ever assent to a loss making you daunt
surmount daringly all fear-made limitations

winning attitude is the master-key of this quest
trust your actions with reaching all you want
consent to nothing less than the absolute best

consent to nothing less than the absolute best
surmount daringly all fear-made limitations

MY DESTINY'S IN MY HANDS

i'm the one writing
straight or otherwise
the lines are all mine

no other god deciding
baptized myself wise
i'm the one writing

life's finally benign
large or on the rise
the lines are all mine

inducing my own rising
and each of these tries
i'm the one writing

i'm the one writing
the lines are all mine

FORSAKEN

it's been awhile since i left
since the day i solely belonged
now i'm rushing back on my way to me

i was certainly true in the way i dressed
for sometime i just went along
it's been awhile since i left

no longer knew what to be
took long to learn i'd wronged
now i'm rushing back on my way to me

i've put myself on a journey to my best
returning to when i solely belonged
it's been awhile since i left

it's been awhile since i left
now i'm rushing back on my way to me

SUN IN DOOMSDAY

concealed in your innermost *helios*
insisting religiously like true *eos*
resilience you're yet to explore

more than a sign of the cross
to reduce to ashes all this chaos
concealed in your innermost *helios*

so intensively burning in your core
all-important piece of your *ethos*
resilience you're yet to explore

what's inside will come across
as soon as you let out your eos
concealed in your innermost *helios*

concealed in your innermost *helios*
resilience you're yet to explore

THE DANGER OF DOING NOTHING

death hides itself behind your indifference
charges for the temporarily-given serenity
extending hindrance all around the garden

you may live a second of serene ignorance
while pretending to be saving your destiny
death hides itself behind your indifference

absent pain now might feel like a bargain
but the price of your silence comes heavily
extending hindrance all around the garden

doing nothing only adds up the sufferance
no even you get to enjoy the alleged lenity
death hides itself behind your indifference

death hides itself behind your indifference
extending hindrance all around the garden

YOU'LL GET YOUR WISH

i'll be the angry-black-woman disrupting your process
you may win over those contented with any cheap fair
but i'll still make sure your injustice is brought down

this bold voice will be heard beyond this diceiving mess
my colossal footprints will prevent any additional scare
i'll be the angry-black-woman disrupting your process

go ahead and disdain the legacy of my mother's crown
you can make an effort to challenge me not to dare
but i'll still make sure your injustice is brought down

i'll no longer sit with patience, this is my time to aggress
you'll get your wish, that i can surely and loudly declare
i'll be the angry-black-woman disrupting your process

i'll be the angry-black-woman disrupting your process
but i'll still make sure your injustice is brought down

I DECLARE WAR ON YOU

butt-rested human being
mind with no question
i declare war on you

with eyes unseeing
soul under domination
butt-rested human being

letting them just screw
drowsy to oppression
i declare war on you

you constantly fleeing
be a part of progression
butt-rested human being

butt-rested human being
i declare war on you

I HATE ME MORE

for creating a space for you
filling my mind with your past
for letting you be this part of me

for never forgetting your bad do
my hate for me is more at last
for creating a space for you

for handing over my glee
losing my future just as fast
for letting you be this part of me

for not moving on like i was told to
with pain looking unsurpassed
for creating a space for you

for creating a space for you
for letting you be this part of me

THE LIBBER'S PRAYER

soul given wholly to the answer of all libber causes
as *mawu* grants thee further breath to stand and resist
be this day another prideful step closer to grand goal

may you never feel overpowered by them olden losses
sun and moon will both avail, be wisdom to your fist
soul given wholly to the answer of all libber causes

get up and do whether shores extend or billows roll
demise shouldn't alarm you, the dream is in the midst
be this day another prideful step closer to grand goal

parity won't be yours, yet victory still *mawu*'s promise
regardless of any, hers the only power that will subsist
soul given wholly to the answer of all libber causes

soul given wholly to the answer of all libber causes
be this day another prideful step closer to grand goal

NOTHING'S GOTTA GIVE

bind him around your obstinate back
quench his thirst with your sweats
and go on being his true hero

put that dream back in the right track
regardless of how stiff breathing gets
bind him around your obstinate back

just like a well-polished arrow
aim straight at your bets
and go on being his true hero

when they dismiss help and give flak
so all know you have no regrets
bind him around your obstinate back

bind him around your obstinate back
and go on being his true hero

BLACK-EYED SUSANS

sated hunger, no longer a growing teen
by the volume of its demands
made full; quiet butterflies

the growling that had been
now a freed song for its lands
sated hunger, no longer a growing teen

lasting hold was not the one to agonize
as result of all the daring cries
made full; quiet butterflies

the days warranted serene
were for her stomach in her hands
sated hunger, no longer a growing teen

sated hunger, no longer a growing teen
made full; quiet butterflies

EARNEST FIGHTER

sprout in lines of loud poems
orgasming the deepest truths
like their poets' devout lover

bear likeness to toxin in roses
dispel ignorance with proofs
sprout in lines of loud poems

compile words with no buffer
to shoot straight at those goofs
like their poets' devout lover

answers for across all oceans
to spare at least their youths
sprout in lines of loud poems

sprout in lines of loud poems
like their poets' devout lover

MAKE YOUR OWN BLESSING

sweat is holy water
the more the merrier
bring out every drop in you

bare prayer has no daughter
for enchanting barrier
sweat is holy water

it's challenging too
yet, go on as warrior
bring out every drop in you

waves' clash will feel louder
and for such hysteria
sweat is holy water

sweat is holy water
bring out every drop in you

FORGET-ME-NOT

have fixed in your mind every single one of my names
ellen was first; follow *ntila* and turn us into proud past
as true parity approches, make sure yours is known too

recognize every insurgent soul and realize their aims
give grace to those that, because of doing, have passed
have fixed in your mind every single one of my names

join in, the estrogenic revolution is long overdue
carry on the fight, so their names don't be last
as true parity approaches, make sure yours is known too

honor *nwanyeruwa*(s) by breaking the rest of the chains
turn each of their belligerent souls into proud past
have fixed in your mind every single one of my names

have fixed in your mind every single one of my names
as true parity approaches, make sure yours is known too

HEAVENLY ESTEEM

you are beyond a mere scar
your existence is no harm, no pain
a beautiful line of my story

perfection is what you are
i got nothing to complain
you are beyond a mere scar

what they fail to understand is glory
i see beauty where they do stain
a beautiful line of my story

glisten like the morning star
their prejudice is their own bane
you are beyond a mere scar

you are beyond a mere scar
a beautiful line of my story

CONQUEROR

awaiting resilience's face
praising high-spirited heart
supremacy that i'll become

overcame life's grimace
now over rain's hued art
awaiting resilience's face

my self's rind is the sun
burning, pending new start
supremacy that i'll become

emulating sovereign grace
as i go doing my part
awaiting resilience's face

awaiting resilience's face
supremacy that i'll become

LET'S BOND (!)

let's not be ones robbing joy
they already do that enough
let's all unite and build-up

our words should not destroy
theirs already did that enough
let's not be ones robbing joy

our hands are not to break-up
theirs already do that enough
let's all unite and build-up

let's give each other some to enjoy
they've already done enough
let's not be ones robbing joy

let's not be ones robbing joy
let's all unite and build-up

WORTHWHILE FIGHT

all rights respected
for the brave crusade
humans seen as such

her voice now too elected
pocket disregarding aid
all rights respected

she can know just as much
no living at lower grade
humans seen as such

womb no longer neglected
nothing to be afraid
all rights respected

all rights respected
humans seen as such

LILY-OF-THE-VALLEY

befit an angel if you'd like
be as pink as you decide
life's a personal delight

we come from down the pike
so you can live with pride
befit an angel if you'd like

don't give in to their fright
free what you have inside
life's a personal delight

prejudice will strike
yet only you can decide
befit an angel if you'd like

befit an angel if you'd like
life's a personal delight

MORNING GLORIES

dressing reddish daybreak light alone
fearing no asymmetrical traditions
giving life to the most fervent desires

now able to experience my true moan
mantled in true heartfelt positions
dressing reddish daybreak light alone

no longer care what their ego requires
threw away keys of my ignitions
giving life to the most fervent desires

finally the one i feel on my bone
fearing no asymmetrical traditions
dressing reddish daybreak light alone

dressing reddish daybreak light alone
giving life to the most fervent desires

VAGINAL PRIDE

each one of your breaths are my screams
paragon once entirely in childish dreams
a universe from the deepest of my pains

you might've gotten lost in life's gleams
but i know happiness is more than seems
each one of your breaths are my screams

a maven that my breast proudly sustains
brought in the midst of summer streams
a universe from the deepest of my pains

from reaching the soul's greatest extremes
prize not even pain knows what it means
each one of your breaths are my screams

each one of your breaths are my screams
a universe from the deepest of my pains

AWAITING SPRING

unfrightened by most-ambitious winds
wearing wrinkles of days well lived
readily embracing concluding-flowers

resigning these eyes that saw all kinds
trusting the new that hasn't yet arrived
unfrightened by most-ambitious winds

still in the day of innermost powers
awaiting the end that we all contrived
readily embracing concluding-flowers

ready to meet the first incensed minds
taking all they too were once deprived
unfrightened by most-ambitious winds

unfrightened by most-ambitious winds
readily embracing concluding-flowers

FOR THOSE THAT NO LONGER ARE

another brumal day said its goodbyes
peace found it convenient to descend
night took your fighting soul to rest

all your efforts won't ever fit on our cries
still your last is some we can't pretend
another brumal day said its goodbyes

no thanks for strength you've dressed
nothing but painful groan at the end
night took your fighting soul to rest

thank you for all gruelling tries
you're why we no longer contend
another brumal day said its goodbyes

another brumal day said its goodbyes
night took your fighting soul to rest

WHEN SHE WAS TRUE

her stiff hair was one of the prettiest pieces of the puzzle
she didn't care for spending the entire day just combing
even when she was the only one minding, she was true

all thoughts were hers alone before wearing such muzzle
she knew her real self despite world's constant glooming
her stiff hair was one of the prettiest pieces of the puzzle

large eyes, beefy lips, breasts quasi-saggy, that's only few
there was never a day she even thought about changing
even when she was the only one minding, she was true

now just being different resounds like a blinding rumble
no longer sees pretty, mother's strands anticipates aging
her stiff hair was one of the prettiest pieces of the puzzle

her stiff hair was one of the prettiest pieces of the puzzle
even when she was the only one minding, she was true

VALERIAN

you're welcome to come in
as awaited by these souls
free to finally just be

no more sweat to pass as pin
refunding aches of our soles
you're welcome to come in

glee goes on a spree
revoking all controls
free to finally just be

once took it hard on the chin
but never strayed from goals
you're welcome to come in

you're welcome to come in
free to finally just be

L.D.F.

love was the cherry of their hope
dancing on top of far-reaching peace
faith led them to a time worthy for all

feared bitterness down in the scope
despite that, never thought to cease
love was the cherry of their hope

loyalty to those that were living small
deposing gods simply creating decease
faith led them to a time worthy for all

from the end of their slaying rope
devotion to reach fair life's piece
love was the cherry of their hope

love was the cherry of their hope
faith led them to a time worthy for all

WHITE CLOVER

don't ever forget those you love
make them a reason why
it's for them too

asperities will darken your dove
and as your body fails to fortify
don't ever forget those you love

find in you strength to reach true
win the ability to not comply
it's for them too

mothers, sisters, all of the above
no better reason to fervently try
don't ever forget those you love

don't ever forget those you love
it's for them too

SWEET WORDS FOR YOU

no soul more glorious than yours
mantled in eminent splendor
a mighty being never before seen

yours is a strength from past wars
beauty their spirits render
no soul more glorious than yours

not hidden behind faceless queen
girl with a heart that's tender
a mighty being never before seen

knowing all that your self endures
to the world, the only true mender
no soul more glorious than yours

no soul more glorious than yours
a mighty being never before seen

HUMANITY

what a multitude to push for
many smiles between cries
too many screams to bear

graciousness to bring ashore
far better existences to arise
what a multitude to push for

devoting long overdue care
to souls before in disguise
too many screams to bear

from the vastitude of my core
human beings with new eyes
what a multitude to push for

what a multitude to push for
too many screams to bear

SELF-BETRAYED

i'm sorry i was untrue to my promise
sorry not having lived sure of my own
i'm sorry to have worn purloined self

there has not been a second of honest
fearing disarray, not even when alone
i'm sorry i was untrue to my promise

the pledge of taking real off the shelf
another word that's been overthrown
i'm sorry to have worn purloined self

but in the lines of a very short sonnet
found recourse for my flesh and bone
i'm sorry i was untrue to my promise

i'm sorry i was untrue to my promise
i'm sorry to have worn purloined self

THEY JUST DON'T KNOW

the pain in the neck for life with no rights
a complete existence accorded no respect
something they're too fortunate to endure

tell 'em the fury of never reaching heights
with nothin' better for daughters to expect
the pain in the neck for life with no rights

futures menaced, all efforts made obscure
delaying ascension for constant retrospect
something they're too fortunate to endure

tell 'em the cost of truly unworried sights
fulfilling a fight where parity is the effect
the pain in the neck for life with no rights

the pain in the neck for life with no rights
something they're too fortunate to endure

NOT SO DISTANT WORLDS

perhaps don't even know your name
have no idea of your personal fights
but ours are realities not so far apart

grounds of existence aren't the same
nothing familiar with all your frights
perhaps don't even know your name

of the gods caring for your frail heart
not even the imbalanced bill of rights
but ours are realities not so far apart

basic human rights is why we came
as i too confront the grueling nights
perhaps don't even know your name

perhaps don't even know your name
but ours are realities not so far apart

EVEN POCKETS

skirts' exertions meriting as much as that of the ties
no pouch half-empty and no exploiting with pink-tax
earnest and diligent engagements awarded the same

there'll be no labia tolerating those acquisitive-eyes
so, just wait for charges of every past enriching-acts
skirts' exertions meriting as much as that of the ties

every last benefit for which there has been no claim
when parity comes forth as the long-awaited climax
earnest and diligent engagements awarded the same

no more time to gratify nor be the scared-good guys
not complaining, bringing down all the drawbacks
skirts' exertions meriting as much as that of the ties

skirts' exertions meriting as much as that of the ties
earnest and diligent engagements awarded the same

CAN I BE ME?

believe the lovely figure before my eyes
accept life's mark as sign of healed past
and actually see her as faithful depiction

glance at the body they dare to criticize
with no shame for its perfect size at last
believe the lovely figure before my eyes

assuring to never believe world's fiction
to give *yes* to the one question she asked
and actually see her as faithful depiction

as acceptance causes happier self to arise
be true, make own opinion first and last
believe the lovely figure before my eyes

believe the lovely figure before my eyes
and actually see her as faithful depiction

All My Demons

core marked by anger
tepid embrace around
in red that's desire

for existence in danger
life in restricted town
core marked by anger

certain to get higher
still with no crown
in red that's desire

behind blaring clangor
a decision to abound
core marked by anger

core marked by anger
in red that's desire

EMBRACE THY SLICE OF EARTH

from this sand sprang thy navel
amidst all an unparalleled grain
a birth conferred upon absolute

don't mind their lessening label
theirs is a life of incessant feign
from this sand sprang thy navel

exact slice of the enduring root
soul with no perfection to attain
a birth conferred upon absolute

existence dispensing appraisal
for its pure value is not terrain
from this sand sprang thy navel

from this sand sprang thy navel
a birth conferred upon absolute

AZALEA

more than cute and forever nice
wholeness that's undefined
not fettered to emblematic traits

widen legs to give soul to peace
fire in mind that's not blind
more than cute and forever nice

strong enough to get rid of gates
but also unafraid to be kind
not fettered to emblematic traits

no categories that'll ever suffice
femininity that's not confined
more than cute and forever nice

more than cute and forever nice
not fettered to emblematic traits

BE ANY

give life to whatever lifts your core
babies, money, be happy your way
work fiercely for your own delight

many ways for a little one to adore
on your own despite what they say
give life to whatever lit your core

if affluence is chosen as only fight
go for it and allow nothing to stray
work fiercely for your own delight

you might not have wings, yet soar
let your own heart be the pathway
give life to whatever lit your core

give life to whatever lit your core
work fiercely for your own delight

BEWARE OF POWER

hate's not the end goal
not a fight to destroy
detachment neither

due respect for every role
safety where they employ
hate's not the end goal

not assuming same feature
ignorance is not the joy
detachment neither

end oppression as a whole
in the new life we exploit
hate's not the end goal

hate's not the end goal
detachment neither

GOOD LUCK IS SWEAT

it does not fall from the skies
it is not given by the gods
good luck is sweat

auspicious life they advertise
has little to do with the odds
it does not fall from the skies

depends on how wet you get
how you face those 'odds'
good luck is sweat

the joy that shines your eyes
like fortune of those gods
it does not fall from the skies

it does not fall from the skies
good luck is sweat

CROSSOVERS

it's not the same everywhere
the army has many faces
differences to recognize

all after impartial welfare
but no two equal cases
it's not the same everywhere

some proving they're wise
others teaching their races
differences to recognize

some looking for just fare
others trying for high places
it's not the same everywhere

it's not the same everywhere
differences to recognize

PLEASE FORGIVE ME

for assuming we're one
for ignoring experiences
for disregarding your own

for depreciating choices
overlooking differences
for assuming we're one

for only considering the known
those customary instances
for disregarding your own

consideration i had none
so i inquire forgiveness
for assuming we're one

for assuming we're one
for disregarding your own

SORRY NOT SORRY

have eyes wide open
now convinced of me
no more hiding myself

no longer playing broken
from feeling sorry i'm free
have eyes wide open

don't wanna be anyone else
don't care who don't agree
no more hiding myself

not wasting time hoping
embracing my own glee
have eyes wide open

have eyes wide open
no more hiding myself

I AM WHAT I FEEL

the sun greets my skin
bringing new day here
and i decide what to be

the blue brings a begin
and myself comes near
the sun greets my skin

by letting my heart see
my truth does appear
and i decide what to be

can't ignore my within
when dark takes my fear
the sun greets my skin

the sun greets my skin
and i decide what to be

BESTOW HOPE

sowing kind words
not singling out hearts
bestow hope all around

like singing birds
enchanting all parts
sowing kind words

be smile for heads down
tell of much better starts
bestow hope all around

there're too many swords
be what heals hearts
sowing kind words

sowing kind words
bestow hope all around

A SOBER LIFE CHOICE

woke up from my childhood dream
saggy breasts, filled heart, and me
never so sure it was the time to be

kiss for me and them an ice-cream
when i saw that i too was their glee
woke up from my childhood dream

dress was a stained apron over me
although took time from my degree
never so sure it was the time to be

as my smile gulped dinner's steam
and i felt those perfect hugs on me
woke up from my childhood dream

woke up from my childhood dream
never so sure it was the time to be

IT WILL BE HERE

the reason they died
along this pathway
propitious times

because they've tried
a truly esteemed say
the reason they died

more than dimes
day of same pay
propitious times

to end the great divide
so none live as prey
the reason they died

the reason they died
propitious times

YOU CAN BE GENTLE

be like bedtime song
soothing all daylong
there's nothing wrong

those lines going long
they are still so strong
be like bedtime song

be gentle if you so want
if no deceit is goin' on
there's nothing wrong

if bliss does come along
only where you belong
be like bedtime song

be like bedtime song
there's nothing wrong

TO THE STRONG YOU

you sob beyond comfort over the hurt
you laugh like kid lost in candy store
there's no one stronger than you

life makes you feel weak and inert
but even when bringing grit ashore
you sob beyond comfort over the hurt

there's always a way to blossom anew
you show by tending to your core
there's no one stronger than you

to persistence and wit you convert
still, while being the strong we adore
you sob beyond comfort over the hurt

you sob beyond comfort over the hurt
there's no one stronger than you

LIGHT

to world floating in night
lost under own confusion
you're it's only flashlight

breasted body in a bright
no any better conclusion
to world floating in night

to eradicate all this fright
to end with such delusion
you're it's only flashlight

you sure are needed light
the conceiver of inclusion
to world floating in night

to world floating in night
you're it's only flashlight

NOTHING WEIRD HERE

don't get any closer
beware of curiosity
i'm not amusement

it's not a cute poster
has its own vivacity
don't get any closer

not brief fulfillment
not for such atrocity
i'm not amusement

no hair on shoulder
still my own identity
don't get any closer

don't get any closer
i'm not amusement

DEADLY INHERITANCE

mine was made a senseless hollow
i was too small to enounce my pain
momma and nana too, so they know

now hear of good chills way below
but only know that i was left plain
mine was made a senseless hollow

a small hole for things that must flow
not even lips for pleasurable rain
momma and nana too, so they know

was told all of them had to swallow
so, my implicit praying was in vain
mine was made a senseless hollow

mine was made a senseless hollow
momma and nana too, so they know

MARIGOLD

afar glistens the sun
seems very upbeat
luckily i also see

after years as no one
as i stand on my feet
afar glistens the sun

saying that i could be
showing mercy seat
luckily i also see

my future is why i'll run
no way i embrace defeat
afar glistens the sun

afar glistens the sun
luckily i also see

MY MARRIAGES

ambition wedded to dreams
from tiring and bleak nights
felicity's surely the only son

all coming in sleepy streams
as an end to intensive fights
ambition wedded to dreams

worry compromised with fun
from moments lost in whites
felicity's surely the only son

life is not as easy as it seems
so, to recover fallen mights
ambition wedded to dreams

ambition wedded to dreams
felicity's surely the only son

SEE IF I CARE

look into my eyes and waste your time insulting
tell me i'm not able, i'm lost in impossibilities
see if i care

i won't convince you that soon i'll be exulting
no energy will be spent on chronic imbecilities
look into my eyes and waste your time insulting

say there's no way i'll ever live enough for fair
and as your lips insist on trying my capabilities
see if i care

unlike you, i know precisely why i'm fighting
so, let yourself be controlled by these futilities
look into my eyes and waste your time insulting

look into my eyes and waste your time insulting
see if i care

WHY DIDN'T YOU SEE ME?

my body was too appealing
no way eyes wouldn't crave
but why didn't *you* see me?

skirt was deemed revealing
didn't know ways to behave
my body was too appealing

if a lady i ever wanted to be
shouldn't spend time in rave
but why didn't *you* see me?

my eyes spread sexual feeling
thirsting for what They gave
my body was too appealing

my body was too appealing
but why didn't *you* see me?

FOR MY MOTHER

você é a minha vida
not the reason i live
you're life itself

se eu não disse ainda
i ask that you forgive
você é a minha vida

i can't find in myself
palavra que te estime
you're life itself

hoje eu sou sem dúvida
'cause you suffered a bit
você é a minha vida

você é a minha vida
you're life itself

STAND OUT

place yourself in life's pedestal
give them the truth of each line
be the author of your own story

be nothing less than exceptional
you were not born for *just fine*
place yourself in life's pedestal

let them understand your glory
let them see all ways you shine
be the author of your own story

be the one you that's incredible
forget the ones that they assign
place yourself in life's pedestal

place yourself in life's pedestal
be the author of your own story

GO BEYOND YOURSELF

understand that yours is not truth of every nation
we're all looking for some sort of stability, but…
in this course, everyone's facing their own battle

see that there are still girls praying for education
others are losing their voices demanding fair cut
understand that yours is not truth of every nation

having a say on your own womb is your struggle
but know some want respect despite their haircut
in this course, everyone's facing their own battle

somewhere out there no water is their frustration
if you can't see, open mind and keep mouth shut
understand that yours is not truth of every nation

understand that yours is not truth of every nation
in this course, everyone's facing their own battle

FEMALE STATE OF MIND

some say this existence is too hard
it's a breath of way too many fights
still go on believing nothin is better

caring for all with no kinda reward
instead, ripped of most basic rights
some say this existence is too hard

looked at like flower doesn't matter
ignoring the place of their first bites
still go on believing nothin is better

this is not a life to be lived scared
gotta be tough if reaching heights
some say this existence is too hard

some say this existence is too hard
still go on believing nothin is better

THIS IS WAR

they're attacking our nature
compromising our essence
this is not the time to stop

there is a role to legislature
let's all assure it's presence
they're attacking our nature

we can not rest in false hope
there no longer is innocence
this is not the time to stop

let us utilize our best feature
this is time for that resilience
they're attacking our nature

they're attacking our nature
this is not the time to stop

REMARKABLE STRENGTH

you may think you have made her nothing
parading such steep and devilish chuckle
but what you don't see is her fortitude
you are still blind to her shining
her face is still mislaid in this puzzle
you may think you have made her nothing
looking at her being as something screwed
like even she was under your cold buckle
but what you don't see is her fortitude
this is one that has long been fighting
but because she wins without ruckle
you may think you have made her nothing

you may think you have made her nothing
but what you don't see is her fortitude

WE'RE COMING

do you feel the earth tremble (?)
do you see history unfolding (?)
a dauntless army just assembled
mass with no need to dissemble
do you see a fair god coming (?)
do you feel the earth tremble (?)
do you think we seem rebel (?)
mere hapless beings just hoping
a dauntless army just assembled
more than anything monumental
do you see we're approaching (?)
do you feel the earth tremble (?)

do you feel the earth tremble (?)
a dauntless army just assembled

ONE WHILE MANY

embracing all differences
respecting individualities
while completely uniting
keep in mind experiences
we do build communities
embracing all differences
to cease the long fighting
use everyone's capacities
while completely uniting
no deprecated references
if connecting humanities
embracing all differences

embracing all differences
while completely uniting

FORTHCOMING JOYS

absolute balance across all
principles of justice fitted
pleasing venues for each
no one else treated as small
regardless if they've kitten
absolute balance across all
from pockets to their speech
in no way inhibited
pleasing venues for each
no more success in a crawl
no one else limited
absolute balance across all

absolute balance across all
pleasing venues for each

CONSTITUTION OF LIFE

you ought to forever find a way to rise
life expects you to jump thy hurdle
you, and sometimes you alone
it'll hurt as if the sun is in demise
in spite of the aggressive external
you should always find a way to rise
scream, cry, do any that ends the groan
no choice but put down the fardel
you, and sometimes you alone
you are one born to revitalize
it's all hidden in your internal
you should always find a way to rise

you should always find a way to rise
you, and sometimes you alone

About the Author

ABOUT THE AUTHOR

In 1993, under the far-famed Luanda's warmth, in the arms of a woman I also called grandma, my first cries echoed, perhaps with no dreams. Solely remanded in an excessive attachment to my own interests. After nine dry seasons, when the rains began, those high and rough screeches acclaimed the artist inherent to me. Since then, every spring has been a way to experience all I can and desire to be.

I am currently the author of six published literary works. And, aside from these publications, I have in my literary repertoire pieces published in a number of international journals).

Through the life's storyline that I have been building with mistakes, eversions and effort, are signs of my potential and gains of my devotion. In 2016, from Brazil, the Maria José Maldonado Literary Prize was the first I received. The following year, Portugal and Brazil honored me again with prizes for my participation in the

Teixeira de Pascoaes Artistic Competition and the 6th Literary Contest of Itaporanga, respectively. In 2018 was the Honorable Mention in the 2nd Haicai Contest of Toledo - Kenzo Takemori.

Ever since I know myself as a necessary piece of the puzzle, few things are as important as the effective completion of my responsibility to society. This understanding has earned me accreditations like the Diplomatic Citizen Certificates awarded by the University of the District of Columbia in Washington D.C.

In an attempt to honor every single recognition and bring to life one of my greatest passions, I found SmallPrints, a not-for-profit organization, with the intent to actively participate in the creation of a just and responsible society for the success of every child.

Driven by what I hope to one day be able to do for it, in early 2018, I participated in a training of historians acquiring certification and skills to effectively practice oral history. The training was offered by the D.C. Oral History Collaborative. In the same year, as a speaker, I participated in the celebrations of the day of Portuguese Language and Culture in the CPLP held at the Brazilian Embassy in Washington, D.C. In the conference I had the pleasure of speaking about "The Female Voices in the Literature of the Portuguese Language." Additionally, in Brussels, I participated in the conference about "Global Citizenship Education. I also had the honor of writing the poem "Éden" which became the song "Rishikesh" of the music album "antes da monção," the second from the Portuguese music group, SENZA.

Every day, the girl who cried no dreams and lived an excessive attachment to her own interests, finds her wholeness. Auspicious, she follow paths that goes from the art of graphic representation of language to those that bring the world closer to metamorphosis.

Books by Cláudia Cassoma

Preta de Vermelho Exuberante
2020 Não Tá Bom
Uma Noite pra Esquecer
Um Beijo em Curitiba
Fim
Fórmulas Poemáticas
Ahetu: Feridas do Género
Silhuetas Poéticas
Piolhos
A Volta do Papai Noel
Amotinação
Cantares de Kalei
The Man i Love Killed Me
Amor, Sonetos?!
~~Not~~ For Flowers
Rogos ao Ímpeto
Ahetu: Vozes Desprendidas
Cânticos de Apego
Pretérito Perfeito
Amores que nunca vivi

Revised: January 1ˢᵗ, 2022

SOCIAL RESPONSABILITY

#DoGoodReadingMore
#CCDGRM

The mission of the **DO GOOD READING MORE** project is to encourage reading while promoting practices of social and community interest. As part of the project, a percentage of the proceeds of my published books is dedicated towards not-for-profit causes benefiting the community.

This Book
___
Proportion: 80%
Beneficiary: Ahetu Project
+Info: www.claudiacassoma.com/socialresponsability

THE VILLANELLE SONNETS

Desert Rose	40
Flourish	41
Amaryllis Belladonna	42
Home	43
I'll Be Right Here	44
Perennial Self	45
Bird Of Paradise	46
Deadly Sin	47
Bluebirds	48
Letter To A Former Exuberant Soul	49
Intimate Covenant	50
All Heart Given	51
Lullaby	52
Be Human	53
Heather	54
(In)Stability	55
Rage	56
Requiem For Innocence	57
True Freedom	58
Crinkled Youth	59

God	60
Somewhere Within	61
Broken Mind In Ravishing Body	62
Orgasmic Bliss	63
Dare	64
Queen Anne's Lace	65
Short-Skirt-Bearing-Body	66
Rose	67
Years Dissembling	68
Aggravated Recall	69
'Til Life Do Us Part	70
Steady Reverence	71
Farewell To Indifference	72
To The Girl In The Mirror	73
Overcome	74
My Destiny's In My Hands	75
Forsaken	76
Sun In Doomsday	77
The Danger Of Doing Nothing	78
You'll Get Your Wish	79

I Declare War On You ————————————— 80

I Hate Me More ————————————————— 81

The Libber's Prayer ————————————— 82

Nothing's Gotta Give ————————————— 83

Black-Eyed Susans ————————————— 84

Earnest Fighter ——————————————— 85

Make Your Own Blessing ———————————— 86

Forget-Me-Not ———————————————— 87

Heavenly Esteem —————————————— 88

Conqueror ————————————————— 89

Let's Bond (!) ———————————————— 90

Worthwhile Fight —————————————— 91

Lily-Of-The-Valley —————————————— 92

Morning Glories ——————————————— 93

Vaginal Pride ———————————————— 94

Awaiting Spring ——————————————— 95

For Those That No Longer Are ———————— 96

When She Was True ————————————— 97

Valerian —————————————————— 98

L.D.F. ——————————————————— 99

White Clover -- 100

Sweet Words For You ------------------------------ 101

Humanity -- 102

Self-Betrayed --------------------------------------- 103

They Just Don't Know ---------------------------- 104

Not So Distant Worlds --------------------------- 105

Even Pockets --------------------------------------- 106

Can I Be Me? -------------------------------------- 107

All My Demons ------------------------------------ 108

Embrace Thy Slice Of Earth -------------------- 109

Azalea -- 110

Be Any --- 111

Beware Of Power --------------------------------- 112

Good Luck Is Sweat ------------------------------ 113

Crossovers -- 114

Please Forgive Me -------------------------------- 115

Sorry Not Sorry ----------------------------------- 116

I Am What I Feel --------------------------------- 117

Bestow Hope -------------------------------------- 118

A Sober Life Choice ----------------------------- 119

It Will Be Here	120
You Can Be Gentle	121
To The Strong You	122
Light	123
Nothing Weird Here	124
Deadly Inheritance	125
Marigold	126
My Marriages	127
See If I Care	128
Why Didn't You See Me?	129
For My Mother	130
Stand Out	131
Go Beyond Yourself	132
Female State Of Mind	133
This Is War	134
Remarkable Strength	135
We're Coming	136
One While Many	137
Forthcoming Joys	138
Constitution Of Life	139

www.claudiacassoma.com

www.ingramcontent.com/pod-product-compliance
Lightning Source LLC
Chambersburg PA
CBHW061654040426
42446CB00010B/1735